GROSS ASA

SNOT OTTER

Discovering the World's Most Disgusting Animals

by **JESS KEATING**

with illustrations by **DAVID DeGRAND**

Alfred A. Knopf
New York

Disgusting. Vile. Repugnant. GROSS.

Gross animals are everywhere, but there's more to these creatures than just "Eww!" and "Yuck!"

Turn the page, but be warned, this book is not for the squeamish. . . .

Gross as a SNOT OTTER

If you're disgusting and you know it, hide under a rock! That's where the **SNOT OTTER** (also known as the hellbender salamander) can be found. Snot otters are *not* covered in snot. But they are covered in mucus, which comes from glands in their skin. This protects them against infections and cuts, and makes them extra slippery and slimy to escape predators.

S'not All Bad!

This mottled, wrinkly creature looks like a rotting tongue with legs, but it is actually North America's largest aquatic salamander. Although it has lungs, it gets most of its oxygen through its skin. The more wrinkly its skin is, the more oxygen it can get through **cutaneous respiration.** Scientists believe that it uses its lungs to control its buoyancy, allowing the salamander to stay on the river bottom without floating.

Name: Hellbender salamander (also called the snot otter, devil dog, or mud cat)

Species name: *Cryptobranchus alleganiensis*

Size: 12–15 inches (30.5–38.1 centimeters), up to 29 inches (73.7 centimeters) from nose to tail

Diet: Crayfish, small fish, toads, tadpoles, water snakes, and other snot otters

Habitat: Clear mountain rivers and streams of the eastern United States

Predators and threats: Fish, turtles, snakes, minks, raccoons, and river otters will all eat these salamanders. **Siltation** (when mud and sand cloud the water) is a huge problem for these animals, as it buries the rocks and crevices they use as homes. They're also sensitive to pollution and must have very clean water to survive.

Gross as a ZOMBIE WORM

Who lives in a rotting whale carcass under the sea? The ZOMBIE WORM, of course! Unlike zombies of myth, the zombie worm doesn't eat brains, it eats *bones*. But it doesn't have a mouth or stomach. Instead, it secretes an acid from its skin, which dissolves bones and releases the fat and protein inside the whale. Yum!

The Dating Game

Zombie worms live up to 10,000 feet deep, on the ocean floor. It's very hard to survive down there, and even harder to find a mate. Zombie worms avoid this search by moving in together—literally. Microscopic males live *inside* the larger females' bodies. Over 100 males have been found inside a single female zombie worm!

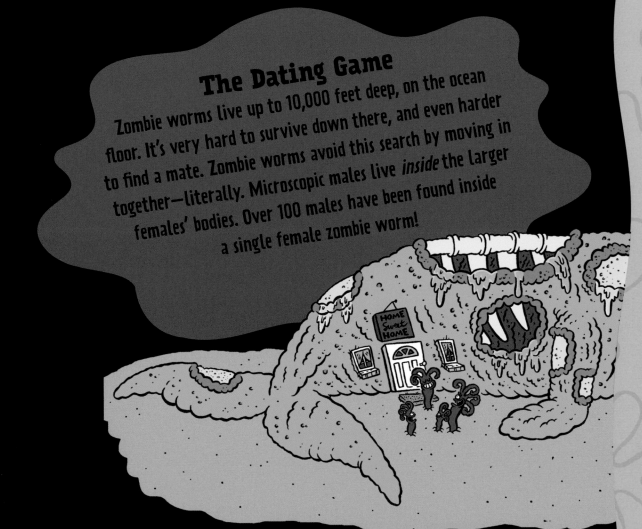

Name: Zombie worm

Species name: *Osedax rubiplumus*

Size: Females are roughly 1–3 inches long (2.5–7.6 centimeters), while males are only about 0.04 inch (1 millimeter) long.

Diet: Zombie worms are scavengers that feed on the bones of dead animals, typically whales.

Habitat: They can be found burrowed inside whale carcasses at the bottom of the ocean, down to 10,000 feet (3,048 meters) deep. Their full global range is unknown.

Predators and threats: Because they depend on whales for food, anything that poses a threat to whales also threatens these animals. This includes **ocean acidification** and **global warming.** Whether other animals prey on zombie worms is unknown.

Gross as a DUMPY TREE FROG

The **DUMPY TREE FROG** didn't ask for its unfortunate name, but it certainly lives up to it. Also known as the Australian green tree frog, this outback oddball spends most of its time in dark, humid environments. It's no stranger to people, and many have reported finding one of these frogs hiding out under the rim of their toilet bowl!

Twist and Shout!

How do you escape predators if you're a dumpy tree frog? Twist and shout! When they're resting, these frogs can produce a loud, distinctive call that sounds like a cross between a squeaky toy and creaking floorboard. But when they're attacked, they scream! The high-pitched noise can spook predators into dropping them, and they will use the opportunity to hop away to safety.

CRIKEY!

Name: Dumpy tree frog (also called the Australian green tree frog or White's tree frog)

Species name: *Litoria caerulea*

Size: Females are larger than males, growing up to 4.5 inches (11.4 centimeters) long. Males are roughly 3 inches (7.6 centimeters) long.

Diet: Moths, beetles, cockroaches, grasshoppers, spiders, locusts, earthworms, baby mice, bats, and smaller frogs

Habitat: The rocky coastlines and interior of Australia, as well as parts of New Guinea, New Zealand, and Tasmania. It has also been found in Florida, likely arriving through the pet trade.

Predators and threats: Wild predators include snakes and birds, but dogs and cats will also prey on them if given the chance. These creatures are **susceptible** to **chytridiomycosis** (a dangerous fungal disease in amphibians) as well as pollution.

Gross as a MAGGOT

Squirming. Writhing. *Disgusting.* MAGGOTS are one of the world's most repulsive creatures, but they are also incredibly fascinating. Maggots are the **larval stage** of flies, and they are some of nature's best recyclers. By eating dead animals and rotting vegetation, they provide a vital cleanup service.

Miraculous Maggots?

In the seventeenth century, many believed that maggots appeared out of thin air. After all, if someone left rotting meat out, maggots were quick to materialize. We now know that flies lay their eggs on rotting meat, and those eggs hatch into maggots. Francesco Redi, an Italian poet and scientist, was among the first to answer this age-old question: Where do maggots come from?

Name: Maggot (the larva of the common housefly)

Species name: *Musca domestica*

Size: 0.1–0.3 inches (0.3–0.8 centimeters) long

Diet: Often, housefly mothers will lay their eggs on rotting meat, vegetables, manure, or garbage, which becomes the maggots' food when they hatch. Some species of maggots eat only dead meat, while others may consume living tissue. They may also eat paper, wool, cotton, and other moist materials.

Habitat: Common houseflies (and their maggot larvae) are found worldwide, usually in temperate regions. They typically live close to humans, where they can survive on garbage and **feces.**

Predators and threats: Beetles, mites, wasps, and other types of flies are all predators. In some places, maggots are grown to feed fish, pigs, chickens, and minks.

Gross as a GIRAFFE

Long neck. Stilt-like legs. And . . . excessive drool? That's right. The **GIRAFFE** is the world's tallest creature, and it's also one of the *drooliest* animals out there. But drool can come in handy! Giraffes love eating leaves from the acacia tree. These trees are full of long, sharp thorns. All of that thick, gooey drool on the giraffe's tongue protects it from injury as it eats.

CHOMP
SLORP

Pee Break!

The animal kingdom is full of gross behaviors, but if there was an award for "Most Disgusting Mating Habit," giraffes would win it, hooves down. When male giraffes are ready to mate, they'll taste a female's pee to test her **hormone** levels and see if the time is right. Icky? You bet! But it's also nature's way of ensuring giraffes' survival.

Name: Northern giraffe

Species name:
Giraffa camelopardalis (There are also many subspecies of giraffe that vary by height, coat pattern, and distribution. Researchers are hard at work to determine their genetic connections.)

Size: Females can grow up to 14 feet (4.3 meters) tall, while males can reach 18 feet (5.5 meters) tall.

Diet: Young leaves on high tree branches, especially acacia trees

Habitat: Depending on the subspecies, giraffes are found in central, eastern, and southern Africa, where they enjoy the open plains, forests, and landscapes with tall trees.

Predators and threats: Lions, crocodiles, hyenas, leopards, and humans hunt giraffes. Because of **habitat loss** and livestock **overgrazing,** giraffe populations are decreasing. Several subspecies are now endangered, and they are also **poached** by humans for their meat, hide, tails, and bone marrow.

Gross as a SIBERIAN CHIPMUNK

Gross **CHIPMUNKS**?! You bet. When they encounter a dead snake, these chipmunks are known to gnaw on its flesh, then rub it onto their own bodies. Sometimes they even roll in the snake's pee. Why? If you smell like a dangerous snake, predators will keep their distance. (Wouldn't you?)

Furry Friends of the Forest

For such small animals, Siberian chipmunks have voracious appetites. These creatures aren't picky and love all sorts of food, especially seeds from Siberian pine trees. When they eat a seed, it travels through their **digestive system** and comes out in their poop, often in a different part of the forest. By pooping out pine seeds as they travel and forage for food, they help grow new forests. Their poop even acts as a built-in fertilizer for seedlings.

Name: Siberian chipmunk (also called the common chipmunk)

Species name: *Eutamias sibiricus*

Size: 7.1–9.9 inches (18–25.1 centimeters) long, from nose to tail

Diet: These chipmunks are **omnivores** and will eat seeds, roots, grains, fungi, fruit, and vegetables, along with small birds, bird eggs, mollusks, and lizards.

Habitat: Forests or agricultural lands of Asia and northern Europe. In the 1960s, these animals were exported to Europe from South Korea, where they were popular pets. Because of their varied diets and adaptable natures, they can also survive in urban environments.

Predators and threats: Birds of prey, foxes, weasels, and cats are all natural predators. These chipmunks are abundant and very hardy, though, so they face few environmental threats.

Gross as a HAGFISH

HAGFISH are known for one thing and one thing only: slime. These fish secrete a **gelatinous** goop through their skin when they are threatened. The goop expands so quickly in water that it can suffocate other fish by clogging up their gills. To de-slime themselves, hagfish twist into a knot, wringing out the slime.

Super Slime

Hagfish slime may look (and feel!) gross, but it could one day be useful to humans. There are tens of thousands of **protein** strands in the slime that, when stretched out, look a lot like spider silk. Some scientists believe we could weave these hagfish strands together to make sturdy fabrics—up to five times stronger than steel for its weight. Maybe one day, police officers will wear bulletproof hagfish-slime vests!

SQUIRSH!

Name: Pacific hagfish

Species name: *Eptatretus stoutii*

Size: Up to 25 inches (63.5 centimeters), though more commonly 16.5 inches (41.9 centimeters) when fully grown

Diet: Hagfish love marine worms, but they will also scavenge marine life, such as shrimp, sea stars, sharks, birds, hermit crabs, and **cephalopods.**

Habitat: The clay bottoms and seafloors of the eastern North Pacific, from Canada to Mexico. They typically live at depths up to 2,600 feet (792.5 meters).

Predators and threats: Seabirds and mammals are known predators, but most other marine animals leave hagfish alone. There are also fisheries that create "hagfish leather" accessories, such as belts. Ocean litter threatens all marine species, including hagfish, who can get trapped in plastic or mistake it for a jellyfish and try to eat it.

Gross as a STAR-NOSED MOLE

The first thing you might be wondering about the **STAR-NOSED MOLE** is . . . *what on earth is stuck to its face?!* That star-shaped appendage is its nose. It might look strange, but that bizarre, tentacled snout contains more than 100,000 **nerve fibers.** That's five times the number of nerves in your hand, and allows the mole to sense its surroundings under the ground.

Bubbles or Boogers?

Star-nosed moles' strange shnozzes aren't just useful on land. Research shows that they're one of the only mammals to smell *underwater.* By blowing bubbles out of their noses and quickly re-inhaling them, these creatures can sniff scent molecules while they swim. This happens so quickly that scientists need a high-speed camera to capture it. But don't try this yourself—you'll end up with a noseful of water!

Name: Star-nosed mole

Species name: *Condylura cristata*

Size: 5.9–7.9 inches (15–20.1 centimeters) long

Diet: Mainly bugs and other small invertebrates, like earthworms and leeches. It will also eat horseflies, dragonflies, damselflies, diving beetles, and stoneflies, along with small crustaceans, mollusks, amphibians, and small fish.

Habitat: In areas of eastern North America with moist soil, including **coniferous** and **deciduous** forests, clearings, wet meadows, peatlands, and marshes

Predators and threats: Dogs and cats will both eat star-nosed moles, as will minks, skunks, weasels, hawks, foxes, and owls. These animals are sometimes caught in muskrat traps, but this doesn't seem to affect their population. Wetland destruction may impact their survival in the future.

Gross as a PARROTFISH

We all like to get cozy when we sleep at night, and the **PARROTFISH** is no different. Okay, maybe they're a *little* different. Instead of snuggling up in a blanket, baby parrotfish build a cocoon of mucus around themselves. This is like a sleeping bag made of slime. They have even been known to eat the mucus when they wake up. Breakfast *and* bed!

Beach Bums

There's nothing more relaxing than a white sandy beach, right? Think again, because there's a good chance you're sitting on parrotfish poop. Parrotfish use their sharp, beaklike teeth to nosh on the algae that grow on coral. Sometimes they bite off chunks of coral as they eat. These chunks are broken down by the fish's **pharyngeal teeth**—and come out the other end as white sand! On some Caribbean beaches, the sand is up to eighty-five percent parrotfish poop.

THE FISHINGTON POST

Name: Roundhead parrotfish

Species name: *Scarus viridifucatus*

Size: Roughly up to 17.7 inches (45 centimeters)

Diet: Mainly algae, which it scrapes from coral on the seafloor. Some parrotfish also help coral reefs survive by eating sponges, which can easily take over their ecosystem.

Habitat: The western Indian Ocean, including areas of Madagascar, the Seychelles, and the Maldives. They have also been observed in Thailand and Indonesia. Various species of parrotfish are found worldwide.

Predators and threats: Groupers, sharks, and moray eels will all prey on parrotfish. Since these animals rely on coral reefs, **coral bleaching**, pollution, coastal development, and excessive tourism are all threats. Parrotfish meat is also seen as a delicacy in some areas, like Polynesia, Jamaica, Hawaii, and the Philippines.

Gross as a MARABOU STORK

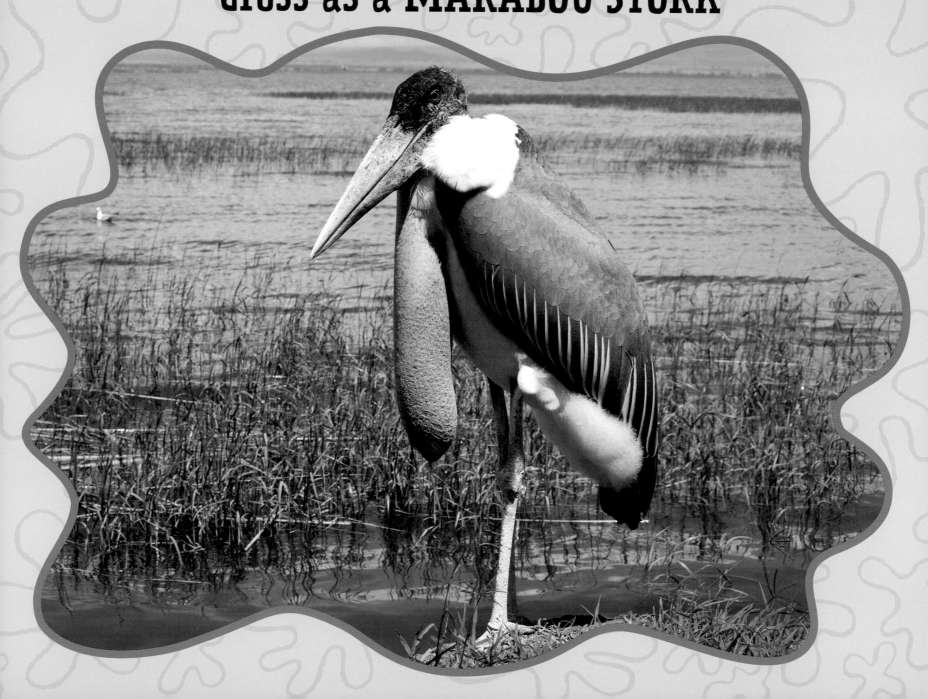

MARABOU STORK legs are gray-brown, so why do they typically look white? The white color is due to what scientists call **whitewash,** which is a fancy way of saying that this stork poops on its own legs! Don't judge the stork too quickly, though. This whitewash of poop evaporates and lowers their body temperature, keeping the storks cool. Whitewash also has **antiseptic** properties.

The Bald and the Beautiful

Many birds have beautifully colored feathers on their heads, but marabou storks have no room for such decor. This bird's bald head isn't just striking, it's downright practical. Marabou storks spend much of their time digging into messy carcasses of dead animals. A head full of feathers would get filthy instantly, but their bald heads are much easier to keep clean.

Name: Marabou stork (also called the undertaker bird due to its ominous stature)

Species name: *Leptoptilos crumenifer*

Size: 60 inches (152.4 centimeters), with a wingspan of 12 feet (3.7 meters)

Diet: Almost anything, including birds, insects, reptiles, amphibians, mammals, and human garbage. They typically eat **carrion** and scraps left behind by other predators. Sometimes these storks will linger around grass and forest fires, snatching up fleeing animals.

Habitat: Open, semi-arid, and aquatic areas of Africa, south of the Sahara Desert. They are also often found near human fishing villages and garbage dumps.

Predators and threats: These birds are most vulnerable to predators (especially other birds) when they are chicks living in their nests. Marabou stork down is also used for some human clothing, as well as fishing lures.

Gross as a SPANISH RIBBED NEWT

You know things are getting gross when your insides become your *outsides*. The **SPANISH RIBBED NEWT** doesn't have claws or sharp teeth, so it uses its ribs as weapons. By pumping its body full of air, this newt forces its barbed ribs *through* its skin. The ribs deliver a poisonous sting to any predator that gets too close.

Poison Stings 101

This newt's ribs aren't actually poisonous. But they are coated with toxins as they poke through its skin. To create the perfect defense, glands on the newt's body secrete toxins all over its skin. Once its body is coated, the newt inflates, and the sharp ribs pick up some of this nasty chemical when they poke through its skin. *Voilà!* Poison-tipped ribs! Any skin that is damaged in this process is regenerated.

Name: Spanish ribbed newt (also called the Iberian ribbed newt)

Species name: *Pleurodeles waltl*

Size: May grow upward of 12 inches (30.5 centimeters), but usually closer to 7.9 inches (20.1 centimeters). Males are usually slightly smaller and skinnier than females.

Diet: These newts are opportunistic eaters and will consume carrion, small fish, and invertebrates.

Habitat: This creature lives only in the central and southern Iberian **Peninsula** and Morocco. It is usually found in ponds, lakes, ditches, and slow-moving streams with lots of shade cover.

Predators and threats: Fish and crayfish often eat the eggs and larvae of these newts. Pollution, loss of habitat through drainage, agriculture, tourism, and excessive plant growth in their aquatic environments also pose a threat.

Gross as a SURINAM TOAD

Here's the thing about **reproduction:** it can get weird. Many toads lay their eggs in water. SURINAM TOAD mothers take a much stranger approach. After fertilizing her eggs, male toads push the eggs onto the mother's back. After a few days, her skin grows around the eggs, protecting them until they are ready to hatch.

Tough Little Toadlets

Many toad eggs hatch into **tadpoles,** but these toads spend their tadpole period in their mother's back. Instead, they hatch fully formed as **toadlets,** by punching their hands through the holes in their mom's skin. One toad mother can release up to 100 toadlets at a time! These toadlets are on their own as soon as they are born, and head out into the world to find food immediately after hatching.

Name: Common Surinam toad

Species name:
Pipa pipa

Size: Usually 4–5 inches (10.2–12.7 centimeters)

Diet: Worms, insects, crustaceans, and small fish

Habitat: Murky ponds, streams, and swamps of South America. It frequently hides under wet leaf litter and is only found at elevations below roughly 1,300 feet (396.2 meters).

Predators and threats: Water pollution is a threat to these aquatic animals. Excess plant growth (caused by fertilizers running into rivers) can make it difficult for them to survive. **Deforestation** is also a threat.

Gross as a FULMAR

The name **FULMAR** means "foul gull," and this animal certainly lives up to the term. When threatened by other birds, fulmar chicks will **projectile-vomit** a sticky, oily substance onto their attackers. Not only does this oil smell horrible, it sticks to feathers and makes it difficult to fly.

BARF!

SPLAT!

Savvy Sniffers

Fulmars have a distinctive tube on top of their **bills.** Scientists once believed that this tube served as a nozzle for their stomach oil. Today, we know that this is where the birds' nostrils are located. That hard sheath above the nostrils is called a **naricorn,** and it helps the fulmar sniff out tasty food.

Name: Northern fulmar

Species name: *Fulmarus glacialis*

Size: 18 inches (45.7 centimeters) in length, with a wingspan of 40–44 inches (101.6–111.8 centimeters)

Diet: Shrimp, squid, fish, plankton, jellyfish, zooplankton, and **offal** from fishing boats

Habitat: Widespread in the subarctic regions of the North Atlantic and North Pacific oceans. Fulmars return to the same nest each year, which is usually on a grassy ledge or on the ground. They also sometimes nest on rooftops and buildings.

Predators and threats: Fulmar chicks and eggs are often preyed upon by birds such as skuas and sheathbills, as well as by foxes, rats, and squirrels. There is no major threat to these birds, but they are possibly vulnerable to big shifts in environmental conditions, such as global warming.

Gross as a CAECILIAN

Nope, this isn't a worm. And it's not a snake, either. The CAECILIAN is actually an amphibian, and it's a dual-ended wonder. Glands in this creature's head secrete gooey slime, which helps it burrow forward through soil. At the other end, poison glands in its butt leave a trail of nasty chemicals that ward off predators.

Skinny Snacks

There are at least 185 different species of caecilians, and many spend their lives hidden underground. How do young caecilians survive burrowed in the soil? They depend on their mother for food. Or, rather . . . *as* food. After hatching, baby caecilians dine on flakes of their mother's skin. The skin is full of fat and nutrients, and, surprisingly, Mom doesn't seem to mind!

Name: Ringed caecilian (it sounds like sih-SILL-yun)

Species name: *Siphonops annulatus*

Size: Around 11.3–17.7 inches (28.7–45 centimeters) long

Diet: Earthworms, beetle pupae, mollusks, ants, termites, small snakes and frogs, lizards, and other caecilians

Habitat: Areas of Argentina, Bolivia, Brazil, Colombia, Ecuador, French Guiana, Guyana, Paraguay, Peru, Suriname, and Venezuela, where it burrows in the soil or into piles of decomposing leaves

Predators and threats: These creatures are occasionally mistaken for snakes, so some humans will kill them on the spot. Burrowing mammals, ants, and snakes will all eat them if given the chance. They are also threatened by habitat loss.

Gross as a HERRING

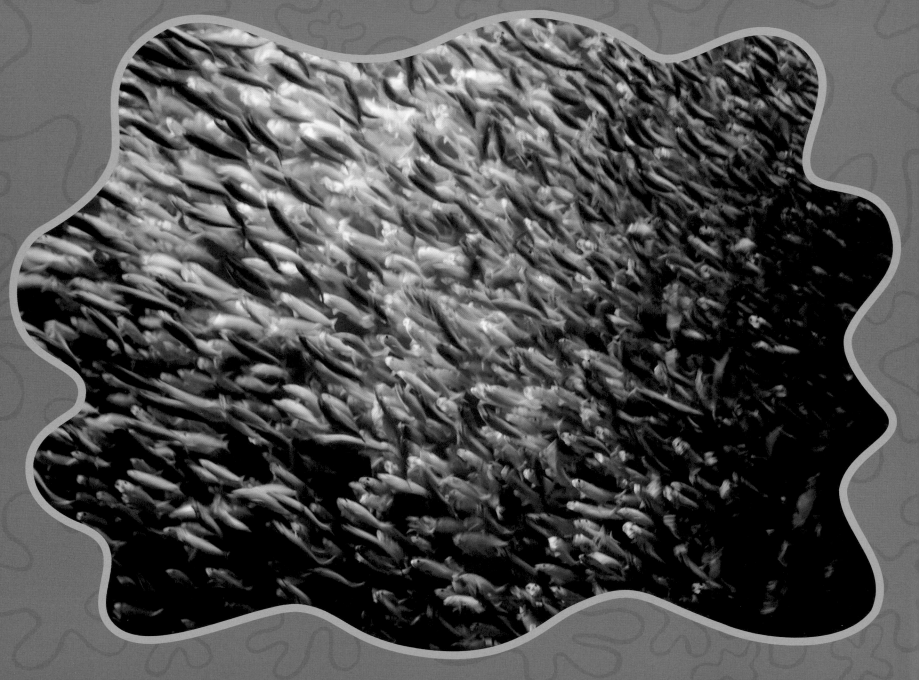

How do you communicate when you're stuck underwater? If you're a **HERRING**, you . . . *uh*, fart. **Flatulence** is frowned upon in polite human society, but these fish fart to make conversation! Unlike human flatulence, which comes from our digestive tracts, herring expel air from their **swim bladders.** Scientists call this high-pitched farting "fast repetitive tick" sounds, or "FRTs" for short.

Whoever Smelt It, Dealt It

There are several reasons why scientists believe these fish are using farts to communicate. When more herring are in a tank, more farts are recorded. Secondly, the farts only seem to happen after dark, when the herring can't see each other very well. Scientists also know that herring can hear these high-frequency sounds, while most other fish cannot. By communicating with their farts, herring can secretly coordinate their movements without tipping off hungry predators.

HEY GUYS, WHATCHA WANNA DO TODAY?

I'M UP FOR WHATEVS.

LET'S JUST SWIM IN A TIGHTLY PACKED GROUP FOR A WHILE!

Name: Pacific herring

Species name: *Clupea pallasii*

Size: Up to 17.7 inches (45 centimeters) long

Diet: Zooplankton and **phytoplankton**

Habitat: Pacific herring are widespread along coastlines of the Pacific Ocean, from the surface to depths of 1,300 feet (396.2 meters).

Predators and threats: Herring, along with their eggs and larvae, are a common food source for several seabirds, marine mammals, and other fish. They are harvested by humans for bait, as well as their eggs (**roe**). Their meat is also a popular food source for many people. Global climate change, oil spills, **dredging,** and destruction of their spawning grounds are all threats.

Gross as a DUNG BEETLE

Is there anything grosser than poop? How about poop for *dinner*? The DUNG BEETLE is named for its meal of choice: moist, tasty dung. Most dung beetles eat the poop of **herbivores,** and their mouths are specially adapted to suck out the nutrients and microorganisms from every plop, patty, and pile. Dung beetles also lay their eggs in poop, which makes a wonderful breakfast for baby beetles.

Stools of the Trade!

In the world of poop-eating beetles, there are three main types. Rollers are an active lot, using their keen sense of smell to sniff out bits of dung, then roll and bury them in a safe place. Tunnelers land on a pile of dung and tunnel through it, burying some of the dung underground along with their eggs. Dwellers simply lay their eggs on a heap of dung and make themselves at home, raising their young right there on the dung pile. What kind of dung beetle would *you* want to be?

Name: Coastal dung beetle

Species name: *Onthophagus nigriventris*

Size: About 0.39–0.67 inches (0.99–1.7 centimeters)

Diet: Dung! A few species of dung beetles eat mushrooms, decaying plants, millipedes, and fruit, but most eat only dung.

Habitat: The moist highlands of eastern Africa. They have also been introduced to Australia. These animals tend to cluster in forested areas, but they're also found on cattle dung in open areas.

Predators and threats: Crows, grouse, hawks, and dozens of other bird species all love a meal of dung beetles. Mammals, lizards, snakes, and frogs will also eat them if given the chance. Because they recycle nutrients, control pests, and clean soil, dung beetles play an important role in their ecosystems. Further research is needed to figure out how best to protect them.

Let's get one thing clear: **SEA CUCUMBERS** are *not* vegetables. These ocean dwellers are **echinoderms,** and they're fascinating from top to bottom. And speaking of bottoms, that's what they use to breathe! They draw in water through their rears, where a pair of **respiratory trees** extract oxygen and send it into their bloodstream. Yep, you read that right. Sea cucumbers breathe through their butts!

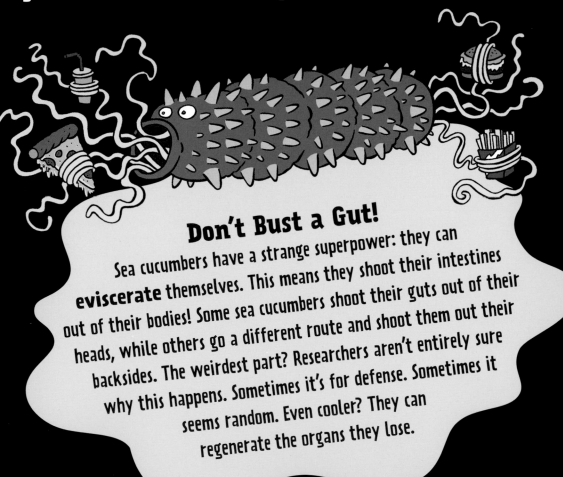

Don't Bust a Gut!

Sea cucumbers have a strange superpower: they can **eviscerate** themselves. This means they shoot their intestines out of their bodies! Some sea cucumbers shoot their guts out of their heads, while others go a different route and shoot them out their backsides. The weirdest part? Researchers aren't entirely sure why this happens. Sometimes it's for defense. Sometimes it seems random. Even cooler? They can regenerate the organs they lose.

Name: Giant California sea cucumber

Species name: *Apostichopus californicus*

Size: About 20 inches (50.8 centimeters) in length and 2 inches (5.1 centimeters) wide

Diet: Plankton, algae, bacteria, fungi, and other microorganisms that it finds in the sediment

Habitat: The Pacific coast of North America, found at depths up to 820 feet (250 meters), where it likes to feed around cobbles, shells, boulders, sand, and bedrock. This species stops feeding between September and early March, when it becomes **dormant.**

Predators and threats: Sea stars, crustaceans, fish, and sea turtles are all natural predators. People sometimes eat sea cucumbers, and they are highly prized in Japanese dishes such as sashimi. Their numbers are managed very carefully to avoid overfishing.

Gross ... but so much more!

The animals in this book are all gross, but they're so much more! Pick two or three of your favorites. If you were introducing these animals to someone who had never seen them before, how would you describe them? What cute or interesting features could you point out that might surprise people?

The Science of "Eww!"

Have you ever wondered *why* certain things make us feel disgusted? The answer might not be as simple as you think. As humans evolved, the feeling of disgust helped us stay safe. It was a warning sign, telling us to stay away from stinky, rotting food or contagious diseases. Disgust alerts us to things that could make us sick (or even kill us!), and that has helped ensure our survival as a species.

What we see as gross can also change depending on where and how we live. You might think it's disgusting to eat an insect, but there are several cultures around the world where insects are a tasty, healthy, abundant, and sustainable food source. And our views can change over time; things you find repulsive now might not seem so awful when you're older.

Is it gross? Keep an open mind!

Do you think COCKROACHES are gross? How about snakes, raccoons, or rats? Your culture, personality, and history may have a role in how you view these creepy-crawlies.

Is it scary?

Is it friendly?

Is it tasty?

Say What?! A Glossary of Useful Words

Some of the words in the text are in **bold.** If you didn't understand them,
you can use the list below to learn their definition.

Antiseptic: able to destroy disease-causing microorganisms

Bill: the projecting mouth of a bird, used for eating, preening, and other activities (also called a beak)

Carrion: the dead bodies of animals

Cephalopod: one of a class of mollusks that have muscular arms, highly developed eyes, and a bag of inky fluid for defense; includes animals such as squid, cuttlefish, and octopus

Chytridiomycosis: an infectious disease that affects amphibians worldwide

Coniferous: relating to trees or shrubs that have cones, as well as scale-like or needle-like leaves

Coral bleaching: when corals expel the algae living in their tissues and die off because the water is too warm

Cutaneous respiration: a way of breathing in which gas is exchanged across a layer of skin

Deciduous: relating to trees or shrubs that lose their leaves seasonally

Deforestation: the process of clearing forests, by logging or burning trees

Digestive system: a group of organs working together to break down food and convert it to energy

Dormant: temporarily inactive

Dredging: when sediment and debris are removed from the bottoms of rivers or other bodies of water

- **Echinoderms:** marine invertebrates with hollow, flexible tube feet, such as sea stars, sea urchins, sea cucumbers, and sand dollars; these animals also have radial symmetry, which means they have bodies with similar halves, no matter where they are divided

- **Eviscerate:** to remove the contents of or to disembowel

- **Feces:** poop

- **Flatulence:** the condition of having gas in the alimentary canal (also known as farts)

- **Gelatinous:** having a jelly-like consistency

- **Global warming:** the warming of the earth's atmosphere, with huge effects on our global climate; scientific evidence points to most global warming being the result of human activity since the mid-twentieth century

- **Habitat loss:** the loss of physical spaces that animals need to survive

- **Herbivore:** an animal that eats only plant matter (and a carnivore is an animal that eats only meat!)

- **Hormone:** a substance that circulates in body fluid and has a specific effect on part of the body

- **Larval stage:** the juvenile stage of some animals, such as frogs, insects, and jellyfish, that go through drastic physical changes as they grow up

- **Naricorn:** a horny sheath that covers the nostrils of some birds

- **Nerve fibers:** thread-like fibers that carry nerve impulses
- **Ocean acidification:** when carbon dioxide is added to the ocean, resulting in the water becoming more acidic
- **Offal:** the intestines and internal organs of an animal
- **Omnivore:** an animal that eats both plant and animal matter
- **Overgrazing:** when animals graze on (eat) grasses and pastures for too long or without allowing the plants time to recover
- **Peninsula:** a large mass of land projecting into a body of water
- **Pharyngeal teeth:** teeth found in the throats of some species of fish
- **Phytoplankton:** microscopic plants that float freely in bodies of water
- **Poach:** to hunt illegally
- **Projectile-vomit:** to vomit so vigorously that it is propelled forward
- **Protein:** a nutrient made of amino acids and found in some foods, such as meat, milk, eggs, and beans

- **Reproduction:** the process through which living things create other living things
- **Respiratory trees:** in sea cucumbers, the treelike structures that exchange gases; they act similar to lungs in these creatures
- **Roe:** fish eggs
- **Siltation:** the process by which water gets dirty because of sand, silt, or sediment mixing in it
- **Susceptible:** likely to be influenced or harmed by something
- **Swim bladder:** an air-filled organ used by some fish to stay buoyant in the water at a desired depth
- **Tadpole:** a young frog or toad in a larval stage of development
- **Toadlet:** a young frog or toad
- **Whitewash:** in some birds, a whitish layer of poop that has antiseptic properties
- **Zooplankton:** microscopic animals that float freely in bodies of water

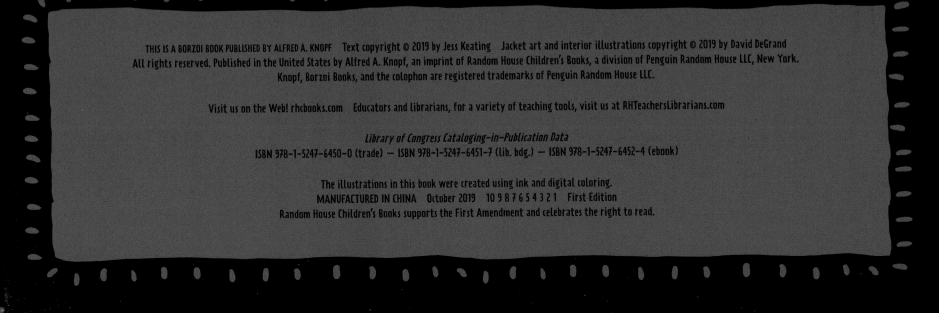

THIS IS A BORZOI BOOK PUBLISHED BY ALFRED A. KNOPF   Text copyright © 2019 by Jess Keating   Jacket art and interior illustrations copyright © 2019 by David DeGrand
All rights reserved. Published in the United States by Alfred A. Knopf, an imprint of Random House Children's Books, a division of Penguin Random House LLC, New York.
Knopf, Borzoi Books, and the colophon are registered trademarks of Penguin Random House LLC.

Visit us on the Web! rhcbooks.com   Educators and librarians, for a variety of teaching tools, visit us at RHTeachersLibrarians.com

Library of Congress Cataloging-in-Publication Data
ISBN 978-1-5247-6450-0 (trade) — ISBN 978-1-5247-6451-7 (lib. bdg.) — ISBN 978-1-5247-6452-4 (ebook)

The illustrations in this book were created using ink and digital coloring.
MANUFACTURED IN CHINA   October 2019   10 9 8 7 6 5 4 3 2 1   First Edition
Random House Children's Books supports the First Amendment and celebrates the right to read.